COLORADO
LAKES & CREEKS
JOHN FIELDER

Photography and Words
by John Fielder

Colorado Littlebooks

Westcliffe Publishers, Inc. Englewood, Colorado

First frontispiece: Upper Slate Lake and glacial tarns along Slate Creek, Gore Range, Eagles Nest Wilderness

Second frontispiece: At dawn Mt. Ethel reflects into a nameless alpine tarn, Mt. Zirkel Wilderness

Third frontispiece: The Yampa River meanders through Pleasant Valley on a crisp autumn day

Right: December snowmelt replenishes frigid water of the Eagle River, near Edwards

International Standard Book Number:
ISBN 0-942394-24-0
Library of Congress Catalogue Card Number:
86-050066
Copyright: 1986, John Fielder
Publisher: Westcliffe Publishers, Inc.
          P.O. Box 1261
          Englewood, Colorado 80150-1261
Designer: Gerald Miller Simpson · Denver
Typographer: Edward A. Nies
Printer: Dai Nippon Printing Company, Ltd.
          Tokyo, Japan

PREFACE

Colorado is beautiful and photogenic for many reasons. With its many mountain ranges, the topography is dramatic and irregular from one end of the state to the other. The breadth of the variety of floral and faunal life is just as diverse. From one elevation to the next, the ecological content of the land changes significantly. The spectrum of colors that is manifested by these life and land forms is infinite.

Colorado is "colorful" and our visual senses are stimulated by it. It is also a place that rouses our other senses. Our sense of smell is stimulated by the scent of wildflowers and decaying aspen tree leaves in autumn. Our minds long retain the memory of the fragrance of sage and the scent of a spruce forest. We also remember the aural qualities of Colorado: the sound of aspen leaves quaking in the cool autumn breeze, or the gurgle of a trickling creek, or the roar of a cascading waterfall.

The visual qualities of Colorado are easily placed on film. The aural and nasal qualities cannot be. I can only describe with words those conditions. Nor can I convey the stinging cold of photographing in −25 degree weather. Therefore it is more difficult to convey the reality of being in a place that we sense for its non-visual qualities. I can put wildflowers and aspen trees on film and make the viewer feel he is at the scene, for the chromatic qualities of these plants are numerous.

It is much more difficult to convey the sense of motion, or the sound one hears of a fast flowing creek. It is even more difficult to convey the peace and quiet of a lake at 12,000 feet at 6 AM in the middle of a wilderness area. In addition, water has no color, or in motion it appears white or gray. Lakes, creeks, and waterfalls are not easily photographed by themselves. The blurring of their motion with the camera can add detail to the flowing water, the reflection of the blue sky can enhance the color on the surface of a pristine lake, but there needs to be more.

The land through which a creek flows or upon which a lake rests gives the water its meaning, both in a visual sense and a philosophical one. It is the wildflowers at the edge of the creek, or the conifer forest along its banks that give the creek its character. It is the moss-covered cliffs behind the waterfall and the steep ridges surrounding the lake that make the water visually interesting (in absence of the sounds and smells and the motion).

The waters draining from the highest Colorado snowfields provide sustenance to the flowers and trees, and it allows the moss to grow on the rocks. Water is the focal point of much of the visual beauty that we see in

Waterfalls succumb to cold autumn air as ice begins to form, La Plata River, La Plata Mountains

olorado. Without it there would be no
olumbine wildflowers or quaking aspen trees.
here would be no mirror reflection of the red
unset in the high alpine lake.

Colorado offers an almost infinite variety of
reeks, rivers, waterfalls, and lakes. From the
outh Platte River's lethargic flow in eastern
olorado to the speed of snowmelt in the
ountains in May, there is a diversity of
owing water forms. From large natural
servoirs to alpine tarns to pools in the high
undra, Colorado provides an array of still
ater forms.

The photographs within this Littlebook are
few of my favorite Colorado water images.
hey are my favorites not only because they
re visually pleasing, but because they evoke
emories of a very special moment in time.
erhaps the weather and the light was perfect
or rendering the moment on film, or the hike
as especially taxing to the high lake, and the
eward was a good photograph. Sometimes the
oy was camping by a creek for a day or two,
n becoming a part of that creek by drinking
s water and washing in it.

I am especially fond of photographing water
orms in the high alpine areas of Colorado.
ction of glaciers has left very rugged terrain
arved from uplifted, and sometimes volcanic
ountain ranges. The precipitousness of these
igh "U" and "V" shaped valleys provides
great setting down which water can flow.

When it drops off cliffs there are waterfalls
and when it tumbles over boulders there are
cascades. At times the snowmelt and rainwater
meanders through valleys called cirques, and
sometimes the water congregates in lakes
called tarns.

All along the way there is an attraction
to life. There are Parry primrose and marsh
marigold wildflowers at creekside, and lower
down aspen trees seeking the wet domains
they demand. Life is very fecund around this
high alpine water and it continues all the
way to the rivers. Here the cottonwood trees
congregate to drink from this well traveled
water. And early morning is a great time to see
wild animals of all types filling their own
bodies with water.

I have pleasant memories of my wilderness
travels over the years in Colorado, much of
them due to the endless variety of water forms
here. What follows are a few of these special
moments in time, and accompanying thoughts
that I have written about many of them.

John Fielder

Along the trail I came to find
A place to which I soon grew fond
A home I sensed was of a kind
Where beavers lived within a pond

Beaver pond, Mt. Zirkel Wilderness

Brave souls will surely try to find
From whence this tumbling water came
Wet rocks are often less than kind
Brave souls do sometimes limp home lame

Unnamed creek in the San Juan Mountains

Overleaf: Sunrise on the South Platte River, near Sterling

Though it appears to be a stick
I'll show you just a little trick
If you'll turn this book around
A soaring hawk you will have found

Morning fog recedes, a beaver pond
near Tincup

It won't be long before they're gone
The colors that don't stay for long
But if you're quick you just may see
Fall colors of the aspen tree

East Fork Williams Fork River, White
River National Forest

The Yampa's known for just how fast
To what great depths are rafters cast
To me it's surely at its best
When it slows down and takes a rest

The Yampa River meanders through
Pleasant Valley, near Steamboat Springs

When autumn comes the leaves they fall
Upon the ponds when gentle winds
Release the grip of aging stems
It looks to be a pleasant end

Beaver pond, Grand Mesa National Forest

They take so long to melt away
But snows of winter like to play
A game of changing lines and shapes
They're at their best beside the lake

Receding snows, Holy Cross Wilderness

Overleaf: Morning light reflects upon Blue Lake, above Telluri

Just before the sun does rise
The red of pre-dawn casts its glow
Clear mornings are the very best
To bath in warmth from high to low

Morning light in the Holy Cross Wilderness

It does not take the flames of fire
To light the land and life around
Of our sun's work I'll never tire
Just look at all the joy I've found

Sunset along the Colorado River,
near Kremmling

The speed with which a creek does fall
Can often be the reason why
I'll stop and shed the heavy pack
To sit and ponder not going back

Leavenworth Creek, Arapaho
National Forest

As spring appears the icy grip
Of winter does begin to slip
The water flows without much fear
It's not the freezing time of year

North Platte River, North Park

Overleaf: Rock Creek
flows through autumn pastures, near McCoy

Tumbling water coats the grass
At night cool air will make ice last
And soon the water will not flow
The grip of winter won't let go

Along Stony Pass, above Silverton

Passage through some old mine
Has stained this water over time
Evening light does stain it too
To make a scene that's great to view

A passing storm, Uncompahgre
National Forest

The trail was steep, the going rough
The snow too deep, but I was tough
I thought I'd never make it back
Please someone come and take my pack

After the storm, San Juan Mountains

I'd like to stay here for a year
Build a house, commune with deer
The water's fresh, the air is clear
No urban noises would I hear

Slate Creek, Gore Range, Eagles
Nest Wilderness

Encased in ice is this fresh leaf
A victim of the autumn cold
But soon this leaf will be set free
The morning sun has heard its plea

along Independence Pass

Overleaf: Frozen pond, Independence Pass

A harmless creek it does seem
It flows in peace, it makes us dream
Yet through the year's it's made its mark
Enough to carve great rocks apart

Lincoln Creek, near Aspen, Sawatch Range

If I was of the bovine race
And wanted just a slower pace
I'd ask my rancher for a ride
Right to this place to park my hide

along Brush Creek, near Eagle

Why this creek's in such a hurry
It flows through land with not a worry
Unless that rain back on the peak
A path to run out it does seek

Busk Creek, San Isabel National Forest

Across the creek remains a bridge
To years of use it has succumb
But if you knew the ore it's held
You'd know it was a special one

Animas River, above Silverton

With such a name one must ponder
The damage done by this small creek
Beyond its banks did water wander
And down it came no longer meek

Savage Creek, above Telluride

Overleaf: Sunset on a alpine tarn, Holy Cross Wilderness